MISTER KING

by Raija Siekkinen
illustrations by Hannu Taina

Translated from the Finnish by Tim Steffa

HARCOURT BRACE & COMPANY
Orlando Atlanta Austin Boston San Francisco Chicago Dallas New York
Toronto London

Far away from here, on the shore of a distant sea, there was a wonderful house. And in the house lived a little white-bearded king.

The house had strange
rooms. There was one room
whose ceiling was a glass
dome. When the sun shone
through the dome, the whole
room lit up. When it rained,
the drops fell on the dome
and broke apart. In winter,
snow drifted down from the
sky onto the dome and cov-
ered it. At night the moon
glided across the sky and
lit up the room, and the stars
twinkled and went out, and
it was all very beautiful.

But the king no longer noticed what a beautiful room he had in his house, for he was a very lonely king.

The house had a library, its shelves filled with books that whispered among themselves. The books of poetry recited poems, and a phonograph played beautiful songs. But the little king heard none of it because he was very lonely and thought only about his loneliness from morning till night.

"Odd," the king said to himself. "I am a king, but I haven't a single subject."

Sometimes he would read stories about kings and their subjects. Always there were a great many subjects, and the king was envious.

Once the king went walking along the shore. He wanted to find himself some subjects.

"If only I had even just a hundred subjects," the king thought.

First he walked the beach to the right. The shore was completely deserted and went on like that for as far as the king could see.

"If only I had even just fifty subjects," the king said and turned around and walked the beach to the left as far as he could, but the shore there was empty as well. Finally the king sat down on a rock and was sad and, as a result, didn't even notice what a fine sunset there was that evening.

"If I had even just ten subjects I would probably be happy."

He noticed some fishermen far out at sea in their boats and immediately cheered up.

"Subjects," the king noted happily, and he began calling to the fishermen.

"Subjects," the king shouted. "Subjects, over here. It's the king, hurrah."

But the fishermen didn't hear him, and all the shouting made the king hoarse. So he sadly went home and climbed in under his fine down quilt and fell asleep and dreamed of subjects who shouted "hurrah" the instant they saw him.

In the morning the king woke to a strange sound. He considered it and realized that he had never heard a sound quite like it before.

"Maybe my subjects are here," the king said and went to open the door. On the door-step sat a huge, furry cat.

"Good morning," said the king with great dignity. "I am the king, hurrah."

"And I am a tiger," said the cat.

"You are my subject," said the king.

"Let me in," said the cat. "I am hungry and I am cold."

The king let the cat into his house, and the cat walked around and saw what a strange and wonderful house it was. The cat liked the glass-domed ceiling, and it liked the poems that the books whispered to each other in the dimness of the library, and the cat liked the music, too.

"What a beautiful house you have," said the cat.

"Yes, isn't it though," said the king, and suddenly he, too, saw all the things that he hadn't seen in many, many years. "That's because I am the king," the king said, and he was very content.

"I will stay here," decided the cat. So the cat settled in to live with the king, and the king was happy because now he had a subject.

"Give me some food," said the cat, and the king went off at once to fetch the cat some food.

"Make me a bed," said the cat, and the king went scampering off in search of a down quilt and down pillow for the cat.

"I am cold," said the cat, and the king built a fire on the hearth so that the cat could warm itself.

"There you are, Mister Subject," said the king to the cat. The cat replied, "Thank you, Mister King."

And the king didn't even notice that, although he was king, he served the cat.

Time passed, and the king enjoyed the cat's company, and the cat showed the king everything that the king in his loneliness had managed to forget—the sunset and the snowfall and the moon that glided across the sky like the fishermen's boats on the sea.

Sometimes the king happened to pass a mirror, and when he saw his reflection he said, "The king, hurrah." And he saluted himself.

And then what happened was that a house was built next door to the king's.

"More subjects," the king said. He went to introduce himself to his neighbors.

"I am the king and this is my tiger."

"Our neighbor's name is King," the neighbors said to one another. "And he has a cat whose name is Tiger."

More houses were built until there was a little town. The king was content. When he walked the streets, people said to him, "Good afternoon, Mister King." On his mailbox was the word "KING" written in big letters. And when he got a letter, the envelope read "King."

"I am a real king now," the king commented to himself. And because he feared that his subjects might suddenly move away, the king gave them apples from his orchard and invited them in under the domed roof to watch the snow and to listen to the poems, and everyone was satisfied when they saw how beautiful the king's house was.

In the evening the king and the cat were often seen walking through town to the seashore.

"Mister King goes there to watch the sunset," people said.

The king would sit on the shore with the cat and admire the red sun, which seemed to drop straight into the sea. Sometimes he would see the fishermen's boats far out at sea. Then he would remember how lonely he had once been, and he would stroke the cat. And when the cat purred, it sounded exactly as if it were saying "hurrah, hurrah, hurrah."

This edition is published by special arrangement with Carolrhoda Books, Inc.

Grateful acknowledgment is made to Carolrhoda Books, Inc., Minneapolis, MN, for permission to reprint *Mister King* by Raija Siekkinen, illustrated by Hannu Taina, translated from the Finnish by Tim Steffa. Text copyright © 1986 by Raija Siekkinen; illustrations and typography copyright © 1986 by Hannu Taina; English-language translation copyright © 1986 by Tim Steffa.

Printed in the United States of America

ISBN 0-15-302165-9

1 2 3 4 5 6 7 8 9 10   035   97 96 95 94 93